American Ruins

GHOSTS ON THE LANDSCAPE

American Ruins

GHOSTS ON THE LANDSCAPE

Maxwell MacKenzie

Foreword by Henry Allen

Afton Historical Society Press
Afton, Minnesota

For Becca, Alex and Cooper with love

Designed by Barbara J. Arney

Library of Congress Cataloging-in-Publication Data
MacKenzie, Maxwell, 1952-
    American ruins: ghosts on the landscape / Maxwell
MacKenzie; foreword by Henry Allen.— 1st ed.
      p. cm.
    ISBN 1-890434-40-X — ISBN 1-890434-41-8 (pbk.)
    1. Historic buildings—Middle West—Pictorial works.
    2. Farm buildings—Middle West—Pictorial works. 3.
Abandoned houses—Middle West—Pictorial works.
    4. Middle West—History, Local—Pictorial works.
    5. Prairies—Middle West—Pictorial works. 6. Middle
West—Description and travel. 7. Domestic architecture—
Middle West—Pictorial works.I. Title.

    F351 .M124 2001
    779'.478—dc21

                       2001022180

Printed in Canada

The Afton Historical Society Press publishes exceptional books on regional subjects.

W. Duncan MacMillan   Patricia Condon Johnston
president   publisher

The publishers have generously given permission to use quotations from the following copyrighted works.

The Old Way of Seeing © 1994 Jonathan Hale. Reprinted by permission of Houghton Mifflin Company.

The Architect of Desire: Beauty and Danger in the Stanford White Family © 1996 Suzannah Lessard. Reprinted by permission of The Dial Press, a division of Bantam Doubleday Dell Publishing Group, Inc.

Night Flight © 1942 Antoine de Saint-Exupery. Reprinted by permission of Reynal & Hitchcock, Harcourt, Brace & World, Inc., reprinted as a Signet Classic, The New American Library of World Literature, Inc.

Wolf Willow © 1955, 1957, 1958, 1959, 1962 Wallace Stegner. Reprinted by permission of Brandt & Brandt Literary Agents, Inc.

Dakota: A Spiritual Geography © 1993 Kathleen Norris. Reprinted by permission of Houghton Mifflin Company.

The White Album © 1979 Joan Didion. Reprinted by permission of Joan Didion.

Who Owns the West © 1996 William Kitteredge. Reprinted by permission of Mercury House.

Bad Land, an American Romance © 1996 Jonathan Raban. Reprinted by permission of Pantheon Books, a division of Random House, Inc.

My Antonia ©1918 Willa Cather and renewed 1946 by Willa Sibert Cather. Copyright 1949 by Houghton Mifflin Company; copyright renewed 1977 by Bertha Handlan. Reprinted by permission of Houghton Mifflin Company.

A Sense of Place—A Sense of Time © 1996 John Brinkerhoff Jackson. Reprinted with permission of Yale University Press.

Harvest of Grief © 1984 Annette Atkins. Reprinted with permission of Minnesota Historical Society Press.

A Sand County Almanac © 1949 Aldo Leopold. Reprinted by permission of Oxford University Press, Inc.

Scope of Total Architecture © 1943,1949,1952,1954,1955 Walter Gropius. Reprinted with permission of HarperCollins Publishers, Inc.

Katherine Mansfield quotation reprinted by permission of Random House, Inc.

Henry Miller quotation reprinted with permission of Grove/Atlantic, Inc.

Robert Frost quotation © Henry Holt & Company.

Publication of *American Ruins: Ghosts on the Landscape* was made possible with generous financial support from Katherine Wells MacMillan.

*Architecture, of all the arts, is the one which acts the
most slowly, but the most surely, on the soul.*

—Ernest Dimnet

C O N T E N T S

FOREWORD BY HENRY ALLEN

8

INTRODUCTION

11

FOREWORD

All photographs are abandonings. Once there was a moment, the click of a shutter, and now it's gone, a framed ghost, abandoned by time and failing memory. This is the sentiment at the heart of photography's mechanical mystery.

In Maxwell MacKenzie's gigantic black-and-white landscapes, however, the moment in question isn't just the moment the shutter clicked, but a moment that slipped by decades or even a century before, when something went wrong and a farm began to edge toward ruin.

MacKenzie is a native of western Minnesota and he has driven uncountable thousands of miles across the West to photograph these ruins before they're all gone—leaning barns and windowless houses jutting up like wreckage in oceans of furrowed wheat and sorghum, architecture that looks more like a visible absence of something, like a missing tooth, than it looks like a presence of sun-curled clapboard and tatters of tar paper. It looks like ruins, in other words, relics of dreams that didn't work out.

America has decay but it's short on ruins. How odd that MacKenzie would find ruins in Minnesota, South Dakota, Montana, and Idaho, out where there's nothing between you and Siberia but a barbed wire fence, as they say.

These pictures continue a theme MacKenzie has been exploring since he studied photography at Bennington College in the 1970s. He's a commercial photographer now, specializing in architecture, but when business gets slow, he heads for his home country and searches out what's left of a pioneer belief that it was possible to become Jefferson's yeoman farmer.

What's there now is mostly industrial farming—air-conditioned tractors with subwoofer sound systems, and huge metal sheds. Driving past these terrible economic truths of modern farming, MacKenzie will spot an abandoned homestead. He shoots it with a Fuji Panorama camera. He has found technology that can print them huge, eight feet long, which is how he exhibited them at the American Institute of Architects in Washington. But when he prints them smaller, they still look huge, because the ideas and memories driving him to take them are so huge in our minds as well.

In most of the pictures in this book, the building stands in the middle of the picture. Surrounding it is land, lots of land, with an armada of clouds above, proceeding through a sky often rendered black by the red and polarized filters he uses to control the strangeness of his infrared film.

Something about infrared film makes pictures feel like thoughts, a little spooky, as if the camera has recorded something going on inside your head and projected it onto a wall.

In a picture titled "Near Fish Lake, Otter Tail County, Minnesota," the white trees stand like wonderfully artificial 18th-century renderings of leaves hinting at bowers beneath, shelter from the prairie winds and the relentless horizon. Up a small hill stands a ruined house. You wonder what moment began its long decline. A leg broke, prices fell, an angel of the Lord appeared in flames and said, Go thou from this land.

The panoramic pictures themselves have the answer: the land. There's so much land, so little house. Everything else but the land and the sky is tiny here, including you. You're at the mercy of land and weather that are merciless. In the woods of the settled East, it's possible to imagine spirits and ghosts watching you, but the Great Plains don't care any more about you than the ocean does. They aren't dangerous as much as they're unforgiving. Pioneers may have thought: If I do everything right I'll be fine.

MacKenzie has found text that argues otherwise; memoirs, records and books about boredom, bad luck, debt, despair; about the blizzard that leaves you burning your inside walls to stay alive because if you go outside for firewood you'll vanish; about a summer erupting with wheat until the grasshoppers darken the sky and eat everything—wheat, vegetable garden, even the leaves on the trees; about a husband who tells his wife he'll be right back after he rides out to round up two cows—she watches him ride around the cows and keep going and he never comes back.

Every year now, country fire departments torch these ruins for practice sessions. Wheat and sorghum farmers fill the cellar holes and run their furrows over them. The abandonment itself is erased. MacKenzie is preserving not only the collapse of dreams, but also the architecture that arose to express them.

The houses and barns were cheap, balloon-frame things, put up quickly so that farmers could work on their plowing. They have a rectilinear naivete, a defiant quality insisting that 90-degree angles and plumb bobs will show the prairie who's boss.

We've had no shortage of photographers making pictures of barns in glorious, weathered color. MacKenzie used to work in color. Then he wondered how abandonings would look in black-and-white, and after a lot of experiments, he settled on the infrared film.

His pictures put you between nature and society, dreams and ruins, something and nothing. How American, except that they show ruins.

For so long we envied Europe its ruins. We studied paintings of Corinthian columns peeking from the rubble of lost cities where peasants and goats frolicked in a poignancy that verged on the smug. (Poignancy is what we had before irony.) We recited Shelley's "Ozymandias," about the folly of belief in architectural immortality, but we admired the Europeans' acceptance of their ruins, of the risings and fallings of civilizations as part of life and nature.

We admire Europe's sophistication, we condemn its decadence. We've tried to find what the Founding Fathers called a "middle ground" of the agrarian ideal between wilderness and civilization. Hard as we've tried to make it work with everything from home-steading to a Teddy Roosevelt investigation of the collapse of small towns to the back-to-the-land move-ment of the '60s and '70s, the dream keeps eluding us, maybe even betraying us.

Hardly anyone lives on a farm anymore—about one in a hundred Americans. Back when more than half did, some of them lived in the houses that MacKenzie presents here. What hopes! What despairs! What wild turns of fortune! The houses are empty, or they're full of abandonment by MacKenzie's artistic reckon-ings. If they didn't haunt you before, they will now.

Henry Allen

INTRODUCTION

THESE PHOTOGRAPHS ARE A CONTINUATION and expansion of an ongoing project begun in 1989. The first published result was *Abandonings*, a book of color panoramic photographs of abandoned schools, barns, and farmhouses set in the agricultural landscapes of my native western Minnesota. A second series entitled *Origins*, first exhibited in 1995, consisted of large color portraits of simple rural stone buildings in France, Italy, Greece, Switzerland, and Wales.

The images in *American Ruins* were selected from hundreds made on numerous trips to the western United States over four years (1996–1999) and represent an attempt to further refine the themes developed in the earlier work. The primary difference in technique is that in place of my former color palette, I restricted myself to black and white—with the aim of simplifying and distilling the essence of these beautiful and fast-disappearing structures.

M.M.

If a building makes us light up, it is not because we see order; any row of file cabinets is ordered. What we recognize and love is the same kind of pattern we see in every face, the pattern of our own life form. The same principles apply to buildings that apply to mollusks, birds, or trees. Architecture is the play of patterns derived from nature and ourselves.

—Jonathan Hale, *The Old Way of Seeing*
(And How to Get It Back)

Near Pomme de Terre Lake, Grant County Minnesota, 1997

Maxwell MacKenzie

Near Targhee Pass, Fremont County, Idaho, 1999

Maxwell MacKenzie

I have come to see family history as similar to architecture in certain ways. Like architecture, it is quiet. It encompasses, but does not necessarily demand attention . . . Like architecture, too, family history can suddenly loom into consciousness . . . One can go about one's life with no thought of the past, and then, as if waking from a dream, be astonished to see that you are living within its enclosure.

— Suzannah Lessard, *The Architect of Desire: Beauty and Danger in the Stanford White Family*

All architecture is what you do to it when you look upon it.

(Did you think it was in the white or gray stone? or in the lines of the arches and cornices?)

All music is what awakes from you when you are reminded by the instruments,

It is not violins, and the cornets . . . nor the score of the baritone singer . . .

It is nearer and farther than they.

—Walt Whitman, *A Song for Occupations*, 1855

Near Pendroy, Teton County, Montana, 1996

Maxwell MacKenzie

Near Beach, Golden Valley County, North Dakota, 1996

Maxwell MacKenzie

*S*ometimes, after a hundred miles of steppes as desolate as the sea, he encountered a lonely farmhouse that seemed to be sailing backwards from him in a great prairie sea, with its freight of human lives.

—Antoine de Saint-Exupery, *Night Flight*

Near Fish Lake, Otter Tail County, Minnesota, 1998

Maxwell MacKenzie

. . . *First there's the children's house of make-believe,*

Some shattered dishes underneath a pine,

The playthings in the playhouse of the children.

Weep for what little things could make them glad.

Then for the house that is no more a house,

But only a belilaced cellar hole,

Now slowly closing like a dent in dough.

This was no playhouse but a house in earnest . . .

—Robert Frost, *Directive*

Near Havre, Hill County, Montana, 1996

Maxwell MacKenzie

Built to code, with 14-foot ceilings and tall sash-windows, the schoolhouses are as formal and austere as Saxon churches. Like churches, they are self-conscious landmarks. Sited on hilltops, so that the kids could find their way from farm to school in all weather, they each subordinate their own parochial landscape, and convert ten sections or so of lumpy grassland and shale outcroppings into a distinct ambit. Bleached now to the same ash-grey, short of doors, windows, roof-tiles, they exude a wan authority, like toothless, deaf old teachers unable to give up the habit of instruction.

—Jonathan Raban, *Bad Land: An American Romance*

On that monotonous surface with its occasional, ship-like farm, its atolls of shelter-belt trees, its level ring of horizon, there is little to interrupt the eye. Roads run straight between parallel lines of fence until they intersect the circle of the horizon. It is a landscape of circles, radii, perspective exercises— a country of geometry.

—Wallace Stegner, *Wolf Willow*

Near Silver Lake, Otter Tail County, Minnesota, 1999

Maxwell MacKenzie

Near White Rock, Roberts County, South Dakota, 1996

Maxwell MacKenzie

*M*aybe it's our sky that makes us crazy. We can see the weather coming, and we like it that way. Being truly of the Plains, however, means something more. It's the old North Dakota farmer asked by a sociologist why he hasn't planted trees around his farmhouse. No shelterbelt, not even a shade tree with a swing for his children. "Don't like trees," he said, "they hem you in."

—Kathleen Norris, *Dakota: A Spiritual Geography*

Near Battle Lake, Otter Tail County, Minnesota, 1996

Maxwell MacKenzie

Certain places seem to exist mainly because someone has written about them . . .A Place belongs forever to whoever claims it hardest, remembers it most obsessively, wrenches it from itself, shapes it, renders it, loves it so radically that he remakes it in his own image.

—Joan Didion, *The White Album*

Near Ennis, Madison County, Montana, 1999

Maxwell MacKenzie

T hose old pilgrims believed stories in which the West was a promise, a faraway place where decent people could escape the wreckage of the old world and start over. Come to me, the dream whispers, and you can have one more chance.

—William Kittredge, *Who Owns the West?*

Near Cardwell, Madison County, Montana, 1999

Maxwell MacKenzie

The great plains is a school for humility. In this eccentric environment certainly one is made aware that things are not entirely in control. The plains offer constant reminders that we are quite powerless over circumstance. A monk isn't supposed to need all kinds of flashy surroundings. We're supposed to have a beautiful inner landscape. Watching a storm pass from horizon to horizon fills your soul with reverence. It makes your soul expand to fill the sky.

—Terrence Kardong, Benedictine Monk from the Dakotas

*N*ow all the heavenly splendor

Breaks forth in starlight tender

From myriad worlds unknown,

And man, this marvel seeing,

Forgets his selfish being

For joy of beauty not his own.

—from the hymn, *The Duteous Day Now Closeth*

Near Hyde, Iowa County, Wisconsin, 1996

Maxwell MacKenzie

Near Chester, Liberty County, Montana, 1996

Maxwell MacKenzie

Worsell wrapped his creation in jade-green tarpaper. Tarpaper was a wonderfully forgiving material. It could hide almost any lapse in crafts- manship. Impregnated with asphalt, pliable and easily cut, it kept out the worst, at least, of the weather and was the salvation of every hasty, lazy, cheesepar- ing or hamfisted person who came to homestead on the prairie. Tarpaper was as important in its way as barbed wire, and Worsell's shack was a classic piece of Great Plains vernacular architecture.

—Jonathan Raban, *Bad Land: An American Romance*

Near Nome, Barnes County, North Dakota, 1998

American Ruins GHOSTS ON THE LANDSCAPE

Maxwell MacKenzie

How hard it is to escape from places! However carefully one goes, they hold you—leave little bits of yourself fluttering on the fences, little rags and shreds of your very life.

—Katherine Mansfield

When family love is displaced onto land, every change that happens there has meaning: the calibre of the light and the texture of the clouds in a day, the big changes of the seasons, most of all the slow transformation of the infrastructure of the place itself as the decades pass. When the deflection of love is also a deflection of pain, the gradual decomposition of such a place can be excruciating, a kind of lifelong torture, and yet, at the same time, a hypnotic, unfolding story. As the place declines, layers of meaning are revealed.

—Suzannah Lessard, *The Architect of Desire: Beauty and Danger in the Stanford White Family*

Near Twin Bridges, Madison County, Montana, 1999

Maxwell MacKenzie

Near Tenney, Wilkin County, Minnesota, 1998

Maxwell MacKenzie

rees were so rare in that country, and they had to make such a hard fight to grow, that we used to feel anxious about them and visit them as if they were persons. It must have been the scarcity of detail in that tawny landscape that made detail so precious.

—Willa Cather, *My Antonia*

Near Cardwell (II), Madison County, Montana, 1999

Maxwell MacKenzie

Montana does not want the ne'er do well, the easily tired, or those who expect golden dollars to fall unearned into soft hands.

—Trade Journal, 1914

. . . *Eventually comes the realization there is really no such thing as a dull landscape or farm or town. Countrysides can be poor or sickly, or the prey of one serious ailment—drought or revolution or the collapse of a market—and it is well for us to know the symptoms. But none is without character, no habitat of man is without the appeal of the existence which originally created it . . . A rich and beautiful book is always open before us. We have but to learn to read it.*

—John Brinckerhoff Jackson,
A Sense of Place, a Sense of Time.

Near Elbow Lake, Grant County, Minnesota, 1998

Maxwell MacKenzie

Near Fingal, Barnes County, North Dakota, 1998

Maxwell MacKenzie

*L*and without population is a wilderness, and population without land is a mob . . . The first act in the progress of any civilization is to provide homes for those who desire to sit under their own vine and fig tree.

A prosperous agricultural interest is to a nation what a good digestion is to a man. The farm is the basis of all industry . . . We must preserve jealously the right and possibility of free access to the soil, out of which grow not only all those things that make happy the heart of man and comfort his body, but those virtues by which only a nation can endure, and those influences that strengthen the soul. This is the safe-guard not only of national wealth but of national character . . . The man on the farm must be considered first in all our policies because he is the keystone of our national arch.

—James J. Hill of the Great Northern Railroad, 1912

t is a long way from characterless; "overpowering" would be a better word. For over the segmented circle of earth is domed the biggest sky anywhere, which on days like this sheds down on range and wheat and summer fallow a light to set a painter wild, a light pure, glareless, and transparent. The horizon a dozen miles away is as clean a line as the nearest fence. There is no haze, neither the wooly gray of humid countries nor the blue atmosphere of the mountain West. Across the immense sky move navies of cumuli, fair-weather clouds, their bottoms as even as if they had scraped themselves flat against the flat earth.

—Wallace Stegner, *Wolf Willow*

Near Pendroy (II), Teton County, Montana, 1996

Maxwell MacKenzie

Near Amor, Otter Tail County, Minnesota, 1998

Maxwell MacKenzie

Minnesota lost settlers during the dark days of the 1870s . . . but thousands remained. Some could afford to stay; some could not afford to leave. Debts held some. Others wanted to hold on to their investments of time and energy. Some held different attachments; as one man explained, "I have lost my all here, & somehow I believe that if I find it again, it will be in the immediate neighborhood where I lost it . . ." More important, he wrote, "I have a child buried on my claim & my ties here are stronger & more binding on that account."

—Annette Atkins, *Harvest of Grief: Grasshopper Plagues and Public Assistance in Minnesota, 1872-78*

*O*n the farm the weather was the great fact, and men's affairs went on underneath it, as the stream flows under the ice.

—Willa Cather, *My Antonia*

Near Otter Tail Lake, Otter Tail County, Minnesota, 1999

Maxwell MacKenzie

igher up on the creeklet I encounter an abandoned farm. I try to read, from the age of the young jackpines marching across an old field, how long ago the luckless farmer found out that sand plains were meant to grow solitude, not corn. Jackpines tell tall tales to the unwary, for they put on several whorls of branches each year, instead of only one. I find a better chronometer in an elm seedling that now blocks the barn door. Its rings date back to the drouth of 1930. Since that year no man has carried milk out of this barn.

—Aldo Leopold, *A Sand County Almanac*

Near Dodgeville, Iowa County, Wisconsin, 1996

Maxwell MacKenzie

An emigrant myself, trying to find my own place in the landscape and history of the West, I took the ruins personally. From the names in the graveyards, I thought I knew the people who had come here: Europeans, mostly of my grandparents' generation, for whom belief in America, and its miraculous power of individual redemption, was the great European religion. Faith in a bright future was written into the carpentry of every house. To lay such a floor as that, tongue in chiseled groove, was the work of a true believer.

Looking now at the fleet of lonely derelicts on the prairie awash in grass and sinking fast, I could guess at how that faith had been shaken.

—Jonathan Raban, *Bad Land: An American Romance*

Near Waterloo, Madison County, Montana, 1999

Maxwell MacKenzie

Winter comes down savagely over a little town on the prairie. The wind that sweeps in from the open country strips away all the leafy screens that hide one yard from another in summer, and the houses seem to draw closer together. The roofs, that looked so far away across the green tree-tops, now stare you in the face, and they are so much uglier than when their angles were softened by vines and shrubs.

—Willa Cather, *My Antonia*

Near Raynolds Pass, Clark County, Idaho, 1999

Maxwell MacKenzie

Near Carlisle, Otter Tail County, Minnesota, 1999

Maxwell MacKenzie

The true basis for any serious study of the art of architecture still lies in those indigenous, more humble buildings everywhere that are to architecture what folklore is to literature and folk song to music.

—Frank Lloyd Wright

Near Erdahl, Grant County, Minnesota, 1997

Maxwell MacKenzie

If we are always arriving and departing, it is also true that we are eternally anchored. One's destination is never a place, but rather a new way of looking at things.

—Henry Miller

Near Kidder, Marshall County, South Dakota, 1998

Maxwell MacKenzie

In the United States there is more space where nobody is than where anybody is. That is what makes America what it is.

—Gertrude Stein, *The Geographical History of America*

*T*ell me the landscape in which you live, and I will tell you who you are.

—José Ortega y Gassett

Near Hebgen Lake, Gallatin County, Montana, 1999

Maxwell MacKenzie

Near West Yellowstone, Gallatin County, Montana, 1999

Maxwell MacKenzie

Since my early youth I have been acutely aware of the chaotic ugliness of our modern man-made environment when compared to the unity and beauty of old, preindustrial towns.

—Walter Gropius, *Scope of Total Architecture*

Notes on the Photographs

Plate 1

Near Pomme de Terre Lake
Grant County, Minnesota, 1997

Awed by this glorious fleet of clouds, I searched the landscape for some evidence of human effort to put in front of the spectacle. I was rewarded by this odd, variegated ruin. Someone had begun to whitewash it one day, but ran out of paint, or needed to return for a ladder, or was called to supper, or simply grew too fragile to risk the climb. I had come to this place because I wanted to explore the land that had daunted my ancestors, a flat, treeless territory that begins on the ancient shoreline of glacial Lake Agassiz.

Plate 2

Near Targhee Pass
Fremont County, Idaho, 1999

The curious thing about this ambitious cabin is the way in which it is trying to keep its balance in its slow dance toward destruction. The upper two-thirds is as plumb and poised as the day she was built, while the bottom, wearying under the weight of the timbers stacked above, sways to the right. Careful to avoid marring the pristine snowfield, my wife Becca and I trudged through the crusty, thigh-deep snow to get behind the aspens to see if there was a picture hiding there. Indeed there was. A gap in the trees allowed me a clear shot at the old girl.

Plate 3

Near Pendroy
Teton County, Montana, 1996

An hour out of Great Falls, the gleam off this metal-encapsulated farmhouse stopped me in my tracks. Floating on gold, with walls, windows, and roof clad in shiny steel, like a bank safe, it had found new life as a granary, saving the proprietor the expense of a new grain bin. A further clue to this transformation is the addition of the two hatches on top, through which the precious kernels are poured.

Plate 4

Near Beach
Golden Valley County, North Dakota, 1996

Determined to make the death mask of this listing shed, my son Alex and I ran half a mile across the field as fast as our legs would carry us, arriving breathless, at the last moment of the ebbing pink light. Setting up in a panic with the sun about to set, I managed only one exposure before it went down—the light raking across the jagged zigzag edge of the door opening, the siding slipping sideways as the structure leans toward its imminent collapse.

Plate 5

Near Fish Lake
Otter Tail County, Minnesota, 1998

Shady groves around abandoned homesteads are often filled with honeybees, and the usual neat stacks of white hives were hidden in the trees here. Curving up to this ruin is a faint track made by beekeepers as they tend the hives and collect the honey. On sunny, calm days like this one, the air here smells sweet and is filled with the drone of bees rushing back and forth to their pollinating duties in the neighboring fields. I walked up to the house to get a closer look and nearly fell into a derelict cistern, once used to collect drinking water from the roof. My boot broke through the rotten wooden cover, now obscured by tall grasses. When I pulled my leg out, a shaft of sunlight burst into the hole, revealing a swarm of striped garter snakes swimming in the slime.

Plate 6

Near Havre
Hill County, Montana, 1996

Here is one of the more handsome examples I've seen of the one-room rural schoolhouse, a commonplace structure that once dotted the western land-scape, every few miles. The puzzle here is the identity of the patriot who maintains the red, white, and blue on the long-abandoned building. The school bell, always much prized and usually the first thing to go, has been removed. I like to think that this one still rings out somewhere nearby, perhaps calling family members to supper.

NEAR SILVER LAKE
OTTER TAIL COUNTY, MINNESOTA, 1999

PLATE 7

I have returned countless times to photograph this house turned granary—from the air, on the ground, in March with windblown icicles hanging from the eaves, and in the blazing heat of August surrounded by golden stubble. Sometimes I shoot it from an angle, showing three planes, two sides, and the roof, a clearly three-dimensional form in the landscape. But my favorite perspective is this: two-dimensional and straight-on, with the isolated structure stripped down to its bare graphic essentials—the elemental "house" shape—a perfect silhouette whose symmetry is thwarted only slightly by the small hinged door in the upper-floor window, revealing its last use, as house for the harvest.

NEAR WHITE ROCK
ROBERTS COUNTY, SOUTH DAKOTA, 1996

PLATE 8

I have learned to be patient and to wait, sometimes for a very long time, while clouds drift toward the empty places in my compositions. Maddeningly capricious, they form and dissolve, unite and separate. Just when I'm sure they'll float in where I want them, they disappear into the blue. In this case, just moments before the sun came off the façade, throwing all that subtle detail into shadow, the three required clouds, taking pity on me, finally fell into their assigned spots.

NEAR BATTLE LAKE
OTTER TAIL COUNTY, MINNESOTA, 1996

PLATE 9

I love this little red schoolhouse. I find it irresistible. Somehow for me it is an icon, the perfect symbol of that pioneer world, with its old, hard ways. The last time pupils learned their ABC's here was in 1948, the date I find inside on a wall calendar. Ruby Hanson, the octogenarian owner of this land, complains, "There were only eight of us altogether—not even enough to play baseball." Now, fifty years later, only cows attend. Some study me. While others continue to graze, several stroll through the half-second exposure and leave only a blur.

NEAR ENNIS
MADISON COUNTY, MONTANA, 1999

PLATE 10

These seven strange little individual rooms, fanned out so gracefully, back right up against a bend in the river—the pristine Madison. A fly-fisherman's dream, the river is transparent and undefiled, attracting anglers from far and near. In this mid-morning view, we are looking northwest to Granite Peak, which rises to ten thousand feet in the snow-capped Tobacco Root Mountains and is centered between the venerable riverside cottonwoods. We assumed at the time that the little houses were fishermen's cabins, let by the day or week. Later we learned the truth. Hauled down fifty miles from Bozeman's red-light district, they had once been part of a notorious house of ill repute.

NEAR CARDWELL
MADISON COUNTY, MONTANA, 1999

PLATE 11

I sent out Becca and younger son Cooper who explained our project to the Powells and obtained their consent to photograph on the property. They told us that their ancestors, inspired by the new refinery in Cardwell, and deciding to try their luck at sugar beet cultivation, built this house to shelter migrant workers. Sugar was a high-priced commodity at the time, and Montana farmers wanted to compete for the big sugar dollars. Unfortunately, with rainfall too scarce to sustain the crop, the enterprise failed almost immediately. This bunkhouse, in use for only one season, has lain dormant ever since.

NEAR HYDE
IOWA COUNTY, WISCONSIN, 1996

PLATE 12

Something of a hydrologic history presents itself in this thirty-second exposure of "Hyde's Mill." A bronze plaque nearby states that the old stone dam was built across Mill Creek in 1850, putting the energy of the falling water to work grinding the local wheat and corn into flour and cornmeal. A century and a half later, with countless farmers upstream laying suction pumps in the river to irrigate their fields and hundreds of additional wells lowering the water table, the flow has slackened, the mill wheel is still, and the sluiceway hangs idle, suspended several feet above the creek.

NEAR CHESTER
LIBERTY COUNTY, MONTANA, 1996

PLATE 13

Here in the northernmost part of Montana—what locals call "The Golden Triangle"—are some of America's most fertile lands. A large portion of the country's wheat is grown here on farms so enormous that their black-earth fields stretch all the way to Canada. Amidst flatness as far as the eye can see, we spotted from Highway #2 a tiny black dot on the horizon, miles to the south, and proceeded to drive a maze of right-angled roads to discover this old tar-papered farmhouse. Drawing closer, we had to swerve off the dirt road to allow a tremendous John Deere combine to pass, country music blaring from its air-conditioned cab. The noisy green machine had just stripped an entire section of its amber cover, exposing at once a billion very nervous bugs. To occupy our two boys while I set up the camera and waited for the building thunderheads to balance the composition, Becca organized a contest to see who could catch the largest grasshopper. Some of them looked like maneaters, as big as your hand. We remembered pioneer stories we'd read, of immense swarms of locusts blackening the sky and devouring fields like this one in minutes.

NEAR NOME
BARNES COUNTY NORTH DAKOTA, 1998

PLATE 14.

Professional cameramen, with the benefit of highly specialized training and after years of experience on location, learn that one of the most important photographic techniques is the U-turn. The West is a big place, and most of it is devoid of the particular form of weathered architectural beauty I seek. After a few fruitless days in a row, there is often a tendency on those empty straight roads to get up to a pretty good clip while letting your eyes scan the fields to the left and right searching for that elusive combination of building and landscape. Something flashes on the retina for an instant and the brain begins a little conversation with itself: "Whoa! What was that?" "Nothing, come on, we're hungry, and we're on the way to lunch." "Was it any good?" "Nah, I'm sure it's not worth the hassle. You've got plenty of pictures already." "We better go back just to be sure." "Ah. all right then, have it your way." So it went with this crumbling barn enveloped in a thick blanket of yellow petals.

NEAR TWIN BRIDGES
MADISON COUNTY, MONTANA,1999

PLATE 15

This grand wedding cake of a horse barn, this triple-tiered theater for livestock, sits close to the confluence of three of the most famous trout streams in the West: the Jefferson, the Ruby, and the Beaverhead. Visible behind the star-topped steeple are the frosted Highland Mountains, and under them hides the old Silver Star mine, whose rich mother lode yielded fortunes for a lucky few. When I saw this fantastic equine cathedral I thought, "What kind of wild dreamer would put such art into the sheltering of his animals."

NEAR TENNEY
WILKIN COUNTY, MINNESOTA, 1998

PLATE 16

Hidden in this peculiar roofline is a rough record of one Red River Valley family's attempts to deal with their own fecundity. Originally a simple, symmetrical balloon-frame farmhouse, the two rooms, one above the other, had ample space for the newlyweds. As their offspring arrived more space was required, so they expanded the ground floor and made an effort to smooth the transition between the old and new. Years passed, more children swelled into the little shelter, and another, rougher room was added on, but the press of other, more urgent business distracted them from any attempt to disguise the joint.

NEAR CARDWELL (II), MADISON COUNTY, MONTANA, 1999

PLATE 17

I could not resist including another view of this beautifully sited but doomed "sugar beet" house (see plate 11) when I pushed my way through curious cows around to the west face and spotted that little log cabin up on the next ridge. The air here was so dry and clear that the mountains, miles away, seemed touchable, every verdant tree distinct and sharp. Studying the old dorm, I wondered what arrangement of rooms inside would have led to the unusual asymmetric window placement, such a break with the traditional order. After the beet crop debacle when no further investment was felt wise, all usual efforts at maintenance and repair were abandoned. Soon the only return on that ill-fated venture will be a pile of assorted boards.

NEAR ELBOW LAKE
GRANT COUNTY, MINNESOTA, 1998

PLATE 18

Discovered while scouting from a powered parachute, this odd rootless shed perches up on blocks, clearly moved from some other location—a common practice in these parts. This was a relatively modest labor. One can't pass a week out here without happily seeing an entire two- or three-story farmhouse, often complete with brick chimney and front porch, inching down the road atop a flat-bed, balanced on a dozen steel beams, with the utility trucks out ahead to let the power and phone lines down. By nightfall it will be moored to a new foundation, ready to be rendered into shelter for another family, recycling of a truly admirable sort. Land is cheap, still, but houses of quality are not. This comely windowless form seems to be hovering over the ground, almost as if it is on wheels, unanchored, ready to move westward like a covered wagon.

NEAR FINGAL
BARNES COUNTY, NORTH DAKOTA, 1998

PLATE 19

I like to imagine how these ruins might have looked in the pre-drought years, before the ghosts took over: glass in the frames, shingles all in place; siding sound and painted, weeds trimmed, fields plowed, cows milked. And what was it like before emptiness took the place of all the people and their dreams? Who were they? Where did they come from? Were there three kids to a bed, as in so many pioneer accounts? Did these people get along, house-proud and happy in their labors, or did constant struggle and isolation drive them crazy? Or out?

NEAR PENDROY (II)
TETON COUNTY, MONTANA, 1996

PLATE 20

It is my usual practice, when after days of hunting, I finally spot my prey, to fire off as many shots as my family's patience (and hunger) will allow, trying different viewpoints and lenses, varying filtration and exposure. Later, sometimes years, after having let the thrill of the chase settle, sober and clear-headed, I edit the take from each subject down to one definitive trophy. But in this case I could not (see plate 3). This angled perspective of the metal-clad granary includes two irresistible new elements that are absent in

the symmetrical one: the great purple knife-edge of the Continental Divide in the distance, and the reinforcing cross-bar that has spun crazily out of position. In order to prevent the house, now filled with tons of grain, from bursting due to the enormous lateral pressure, several steel cables have been strung across the interior and are anchored to the beams outside. Recycled dwellings are deemed superior storehouses over round metal grain bins because the wood breathes, preventing spoilage of the outermost layer of grain from condensation.

NEAR AMOR
OTTER TAIL COUNTY, MINNESOTA, 1998

PLATE 21

I make a yearly pilgrimage to this Minnesota ruin, documenting its slow slide into nothingness. Since the previous August, it's become a little less solid, a bit more transparent. More shingles have blown off; more boards have sprung loose, flopped onto the corrupting ground, and begun their vanishing act. Although enough roof still remains to shed most of the rain and snow, one day, my beard white, I may return to find only the concrete silo standing. On this particular evening, there were two races to run: first, to expose the film before the speeding shadow flew out of the frame; and second, to pack up and hump it back across the darkening meadow to the safety of the truck before ferocious mobs of mosquitoes sucked my every last drop of blood.

NEAR OTTER TAIL LAKE
OTTER TAIL COUNTY, MINNESOTA, 1999

PLATE 22

This stable, surrounded by a quarter-section of yellow-green vegetation, is invisible from any road, at least in summer. As was the rule in these parts, a "shelterbelt" of trees had been planted around the property to gain some protection from powerful "Alberta Clippers." I drove by for over forty years and never knew it was there, just past the barrier of evergreens and oaks, only five minutes down the lane from the lake and my grandfather's cottage. It came as quite a delicious surprise, while flying around the lake in a powered parachute, to discover so close to home such a feast for the eyes. When I returned by foot the following morning, the sky was clear, but as I set up the tripod, a few cottony cumuli, tumbling in from the west, began building. Soon they thickened and bubbled above the barn, perfecting a tasty layer cake of textures: sky, clouds, trees, and sorghum.

NEAR DODGEVILLE
IOWA COUNTY, WISCONSIN, 1996

PLATE 23

To acquire some "atmospheric" background images for their catalogs, a well-known company hired me to see what ruins I could find in the area surrounding their headquarters. Setting off in my rental car for a week of shooting, with high hopes for delivering a collection of beautiful, nostalgic, and useful images, I soon discovered, to my dismay, that the Dodgeville region is lush, prosperous, fertile, and well watered. There had been no droughts, no plagues of locusts, no wholesale abandonment of farms. Not surprising. The pioneers here had first choice. They liked these emerald hills and stayed. One of the few untended derelicts I found was this sturdy grizzled barn, balanced on boulders, still master of all it surveys.

NEAR WATERLOO
MADISON COUNTY, MONTANA, 1999

PLATE 24

Having captured many examples of the early pioneer homestead in the Great Plains, I traveled here with the specific aim of depicting its counterpart with the backdrop of the Rockies. This ideal vision of the quintessential log home was spotted from a little dirt track that runs along those trees at the base of the Tobacco Root Mountains. The light was still on the featureless east façade, facing me, and I knew that, for a change, I would have time to hike leisurely across the pasture before the sun moved around to the west face, its single door the only penetration in the cabin's long umber wall. In an effort to place the structure entirely below the ridgeline, I kept backing up the camera until I ran out of ground. I made this view with my tripod set up inches from the steep bank of the Jefferson River which connected these settlers by canoe with the other riverside homesteads and then, like Lewis and Clark, down the great Missouri through the Dakotas to St. Louis.

NEAR RAYNOLDS PASS
CLARK COUNTY, IDAHO, 1999

PLATE 25

The question here is, why did this roof collapse into such a striking geometric grid, black squares drawn against the sky like a giant's tick-tack-toe game? The answer probably lies in the limitations of both the construction techniques and materials available at the time. Unable to obtain (or afford) milled lumber in one long piece, the builder spliced the ridgepole from two shorter lengths and overlapped them in the middle, creating a fatal fault in the structure. His jerry-built joint eventually gave way under the weight of the snow, and the back of this otherwise sound cabin broke. Ironically, the builder was clearly aware that, other than the one required door, every additional cut in his massive log walls would weaken them. So he did without the rich man's luxury of windows, creating quite a cozy, restful cabin, unencumbered by excessive daylight.

NEAR CARLISLE
OTTER TAIL COUNTY, MINNESOTA, 1999

PLATE 26

Most of the one-room schoolhouses in Otter Tail County were sold to neighboring landowners in the forties and fifties when the orange buses starting taking postwar baby-boom kids to the new centralized town schools. Many old schools simply fell down or were dismantled. Fortunately, some were converted to new uses such as township halls or as "starter homes," a more graceful alternative to the ubiquitous "mobile" home. I once tracked down a schoolhouse graced with two little doors marked "Boys" and "Girls" that had been hoisted up and trucked to the next county to begin a new life as a (coed) chicken coop. This one was moved here by a sentimental graduate who was just rather fond of it.

NEAR ERDAHL
GRANT COUNTY, MINNESOTA, 1997

PLATE 27

I would have passed by this unremarkable little shed but for the elliptical shadow betraying the otherwise invisible rusted, netless basketball hoop, unmistakable evidence of a restless teenage boy, now long since run off to "the Cities" to escape the fate he felt encircling him.

NEAR KIDDER
MARSHALL COUNTY, SOUTH DAKOTA, 1998

PLATE 28

Unusually short, minus the customary bell tower, its roof pitch curiously squat, this austere colorless structure is a most humble example of the one-room schoolhouse. Merely fifteen by twenty feet, it was thrown up in haste one summer to shelter the new teacher coming from out East and a half dozen assorted farm kids. This part of the Dakotas, with more people giving up every year, is now so scarcely populated that I could set up my camera in the middle of the road with impunity. The charm of this lonely structure, for me, comes from the vestibule, a requirement in this unforgiving climate, its miniature gable a graceful echo of the main roof.

NEAR HEBGEN LAKE
GALLATIN COUNTY, MONTANA, 1999

PLATE 29

We arrived too late to document the log barn whose scattered remains penetrate the foreground snow. Because it was built earlier, or less well, the brutal blizzards of this high plateau pulled it down decades ago. Although our map claimed a large lake filled this valley, we could not detect its frozen shore, now indistinguishable from the bleak terrain surrounding it. On a gold summer afternoon this spot must be idyllic, with its agreeable prospect over the water to the mountains. But on this frigid morning, with icicles hanging from my beard, it was hard to imagine that anyone could survive a winter in this place.

NEAR WEST YELLOWSTONE
GALLATIN COUNTY, MONTANA, 1999

PLATE 30

Having fallen into the practice of picturing the building small in the large landscape, I tried the opposite approach with this deserted cabin, just outside Yellowstone National Park. Amidst ancient appliances and junked pickups, its surroundings stymied my standard view, so this portrait focuses on the cabin's face, savoring the character of the rough-hewn logs. Peering through the broken window frames into the blackness, I was thankful for the scoundrel who scavenged both the front and back doors, leaving behind this glimpse of the snowy hillside beyond.

SOME TECHNICAL NOTES ABOUT THE ORIGINAL PHOTOGRAPHS REPRODUCED IN THIS MONOGRAPH

All photographs were made with either the Fuji Panorama "G617" or "GX617" extra-wide format cameras, using Konica Black & White Infrared 750 film, with deep red and polarizing filters. With these cameras, each roll yields four panoramic images—with a height-to-width ratio of 1–to–3. As the camera back must be opened up to place a ground glass on the film plane for composing—before making each new view, a minimum of one roll (four bracketed exposures) was exposed for each subject.

Each print reproduced for this book was projection printed by hand directly from the original 6 x 17 cm (approximately 2 1/4″ x 7″) black & white negatives. In all cases the entire negative is shown exactly as exposed, without cropping or retouching. There have been no digital processes involved in the production of the original work, nor have any computer correction or manipulations (Photoshop) been employed. The original photographs are archivally processed silver gelatin prints and are in signed, limited editions of 20 and 50.

M.M.

EXHIBITIONS
AWARDS
COLLECTIONS

ONE MAN EXHIBITIONS

American Institute of Architects, Washington, DC - 2000, 1995, 1993

Anne Reed Gallery, Sun Valley, Idaho - 2000

Virginia Foundation for Architecture, Richmond, VA - 2000, 1996, 1994

Humanities Fine Arts Gallery, University of Minnesota, Morris, MN - 1999

Minnesota State Capitol, St. Paul, MN - 1999

Center for the Arts, Fergus Falls, MN - 1999

Julie Saul Gallery, New York, NY - 1997, 1994

Bivins Gallery, Institute of the Arts, Duke University, Durham, NC - 1996

Addison/Ripley Gallery, Washington, DC - 1995

AWARDS

2000 - Graham Foundation for Advanced Studies in the Arts grant awarded for photography project "Tobacco Barns"

2000 - District of Columbia Commission on the Arts and Humanities and the National Endowment for the Arts, Individual Artists Fellowship grant

1996 - *Photo District News*, Silver Medal Award for Excellence for the book, *Abandonings, Photographs of Otter Tail County, Minnesota*, by Maxwell MacKenzie, published by Elliott & Clark, 1995

1994 - The Virginia Society of the American Institute of Architects, Certificate of Honor recognizing Contribution to Architecture in Virginia

SELECTED CORPORATE AND INSTITUTIONAL COLLECTIONS

American Embassy, US Department of State, Bogota, Colombia

American Embassy, US Department of State, Lima, Peru

The American Architectural Foundation, Washington, DC

Bennington College, President's Collection, Bennington, VT

Brown & Wood, New York, NY

Bumper Development, Calgary, Canada

Cadwalader, Wickersham & Taft, Washington, DC

Carey Ellis, Dallas, TX

Carnemark Systems & Design, Bethesda, MD

Citibank—Private Banking, London, England

Columbia Presbyterian Hospital, New York, NY

Columbus Regional Hospital, Columbus, IN

Deloitte & Touche, Washington, DC

Dow Jones, New York, NY

Exxon Corporation, New York, NY

Fannie May, Washington, DC

Flemming, Zulack & Williamson, New York, NY

Gibson Creative, Washington, DC

Goldman Sachs, New York, NY

Group C, New Haven, CT

Hewitt, Magnard & Kristal, New York, NY

Johnson & Johnson, New York, NY

J.W. Kaempfer, London, England

K-Medic, Inc., New York, NY

J.P. Morgan, New York, NY

Muir, Costello & Carlson, Lakefield, MN

New York Hospital, New York, NY

Octagon Museum, Washington, DC

Orrick, Herrington & Sutcliffe, New York, NY

The Otter Tail County Historical Museum, Fergus Falls, MN

St. Albans School, Washington, DC

Stein, Roe & Farnham, New York, NY

Steen Hamilton, New York, NY

Wachtel, Lipton, Rosen & Katz, New York, NY

Union Bank of Switzerland

The *Washington Post,* Washington, DC

Weiner, Brodsky, Sidman & Kider, Washington, DC

Designed by
Barbara J. Arney
Stillwater, Minnesota

Typefaces are
Mistral
Berkeley Book
Berkeley Italic